Heaven

Eugen

methuen | drama

LONDON • NEW YORK • OXFORD • NEW DELHI • SYDNEY

METHUEN DRAMA
Bloomsbury Publishing Plc
50 Bedford Square, London, WC1B 3DP, UK
1385 Broadway, New York, NY 10018, USA
29 Earlsfort Terrace, Dublin 2, Ireland

BLOOMSBURY, METHUEN DRAMA and the Methuen
Drama logo are trademarks of Bloomsbury Publishing Plc

First published in Great Britain 2022

Copyright © Eugene O'Brien, 2022

Eugene O'Brien has asserted his right under the Copyright, Designs
and Patents Act, 1988, to be identified as author of this work.

For legal purposes the Acknowledgements on p. viii
constitute an extension of this copyright page.

Cover image by Leo Byrne & Publicis

All rights reserved. No part of this publication may be reproduced or
transmitted in any form or by any means, electronic or mechanical, including
photocopying, recording, or any information storage or retrieval system,
without prior permission in writing from the publishers.

Bloomsbury Publishing Plc does not have any control over, or responsibility
for, any third-party websites referred to or in this book. All internet addresses
given in this book were correct at the time of going to press. The author and
publisher regret any inconvenience caused if addresses have changed or sites
have ceased to exist, but can accept no responsibility for any such changes.

No rights in incidental music or songs contained in the work are hereby
granted and performance rights for any performance and/or presentation
whatsoever must be obtained from the respective copyright owners.

All rights whatsoever in this play are strictly reserved and application
for performance etc. should be made before rehearsals to Curtis Brown
Group Ltd., Haymarket House, 28–29 Haymarket, London, SW1Y 4SP.
No performance may be given unless a licence has been obtained.

A catalogue record for this book is available from the British Library.

A catalog record for this book is available from the Library of Congress.

ISBN: PB: 978-1-3503-5664-1
ePDF: 978-1-3503-5665-8
eBook: 978-1-3503-5666-5

Series: Modern Plays

Typeset by Mark Heslington Ltd, Scarborough, North Yorkshire
Printed and bound in Great Britain

To find out more about our authors and books visit
www.bloomsbury.com and sign up for our newsletters.

ABOUT FISHAMBLE

Fishamble is an Irish theatre company that discovers, develops and produces new plays of national importance with a global reach. It has toured its productions to audiences throughout Ireland, and to 19 other countries. It champions the role of the playwright, typically supporting over 50% of the writers of all new plays produced on the island of Ireland each year. Fishamble has received many awards in Ireland and internationally, including an Olivier Award.

'the much-loved Fishamble [is] a global brand with international theatrical presence . . . an unswerving force for new writing' *Irish Times*

'Ireland's leading new writing company' *The Stage*

'the respected Dublin company . . . forward-thinking Fishamble' *New York Times*

'excellent Fishamble . . . Ireland's terrific Fishamble' *The Guardian*

'when Fishamble is [in New York], you've got to go' *Time Out New York*

'that great Irish new writing company, Fishamble' Lyn Gardner, *Stage Door*

'Fishamble puts electricity into the National grid of dreams' *Sebastian Barry*

Fishamble Staff: Jim Culleton (Artistic Director & CEO), Eva Scanlan (Executive Director), Gavin Kostick (Literary Manager), Ronan Carey (Office & Production Coordinator), Freya Gillespie (Fundraising & Development Executive), Cally Shine (Associate Producer), Dafni Zarkadi (Marketing Officer)

Fishamble Board: Peter Finnegan, John McGrane, Louise Molloy, Doireann Ní Bhriain (Chair), Ronan Nulty, John

O'Donnell, Siobhan O'Leary (Vice Chair), Colleen Savage, John Tierney

Fishamble is funded by the Arts Council, Dublin City Council and Culture Ireland.

Fishamble's recent and current productions include:

- *Outrage* by Deirdre Kinahan (2022) touring and online, as part of the Decade of Centenaries
- *The Pride of Parnell Street* by Sebastian Barry (2007–11, and 2022) touring in Ireland and internationally, BBC Audio
- *The Treaty* by Colin Murphy (2021–2) in Ireland, Irish Embassy in London, and online as part of the Decade of Centenaries and Seoda Festival
- *Duck Duck Goose* by Caitríona Daly (2021–2) touring in Ireland and online
- *On Blueberry Hill* by Sebastian Barry (2017–21) touring in Ireland, Europe, Off-Broadway, West End, Audible and online
- *Before* by Pat Kinevane (since 2018) touring in Ireland, internationally, and online, as well as a bilingual version Before/Sula
- *Mustard* by Eva O'Connor (since 2020) on tour in Ireland, internationally and online
- *On the Horizon* in association with Dirty Protest, by Shannon Yee, Hefin Robinson, Michael Patrick, Oisín Kearney, Samantha O'Rourke, Ciara Elizabeth Smyth, Connor Allen (2021) online
- *Tiny Plays for a Brighter Future* by Niall Murphy, Signe Lury, Eva-Jane Gaffney (2021) online

- *Embargo* by Deirdre Kinahan (2020) online during Dublin Theatre Festival
- *Tiny Plays 24/7* by Lora Hartin, Maria Popovic, Ciara Elizabeth Smyth, Caitríona Daly, Conor Hanratty, Julia Marks, Patrick O'Laoghaire, Eric O'Brien, Grace Lobo, Ryan Murphy (2020) online
- *The Alternative* by Oisín Kearney and Michael Patrick (2019) on tour to Pavilion Theatre, Draíocht, Belltable, Everyman Theatre, Town Hall Theatre and Lyric Theatre
- *Haughey | Gregory* by Colin Murphy (2018–19) in the Abbey Theatre, Mountjoy Prison, Dáil Éireann, Croke Park and Larkin Community College, as well as on national tour
- *The Humours of Bandon* by Margaret McAuliffe (2017–19) touring in Ireland, UK, US and Australia
- *Rathmines Road* by Deirdre Kinahan (2018) in coproduction with the Abbey Theatre
- *Drip Feed* by Karen Cogan (2018) in coproduction with Soho Theatre, touring in Ireland and UK
- *GPO 1818* by Colin Murphy (2018) to mark the bicentenary of the GPO
- *Maz & Bricks* by Eva O'Connor (2017–18) on national and international tour
- *Forgotten, Silent and Underneath* by Pat Kinevane (since 2007, 2011 and 2014, respectively) touring in Ireland, UK, Europe, US, Australia, New Zealand and online
- *Charolais* by Noni Stapleton (2017) in New York
- *Inside the GPO* by Colin Murphy (2016) performed in the GPO during Easter
- *Tiny Plays for Ireland and America* by 26 writers (2016) at the Kennedy Center, Washington, DC, and Irish Arts Center, New York, as part of Ireland 100
- *Mainstream* by Rosaleen McDonagh (2016) in coproduction with Project Arts Centre
- *Invitation to a Journey* by David Bolger, Deirdre Gribbin and Gavin Kostick (2016) in coproduction with

CoisCeim, Crash Ensemble and Galway International Arts Festival

- *Little Thing, Big Thing* by Donal O'Kelly (2014–16) touring in Ireland, UK, Europe, US and Australia
- *Swing* by Steve Blount, Peter Daly, Gavin Kostick and Janet Moran (2014–16) touring in Ireland, UK, Europe, US, Australia and New Zealand
- *Bailed Out* by Colin Murphy (2015) on national tour
- *Spinning* by Deirdre Kinahan (2014) at Dublin Theatre Festival
- *The Wheelchair on My Face* by Sonya Kelly (2013–14) touring in Ireland, UK, Europe and US.

Fishamble wishes to thank the following Friends of Fishamble & Corporate Members for their invaluable support:

Alan Ashe, ATM Accounting Services, Mary Banotti, Tania Banotti, Grainne Holmes Blumenthal, Doireann Ní Bhriain, Colette and Barry Breen, Sean Brett, John Butler, Betsy Carroll, Breda Cashe, Barry Cassidy, Maura Connolly, Finola Earley, J. Fitzgibbon John & Yvonne Healy, Alison Howard, Geoffrey & Jane Keating, Stephen Lambert, Damian Lane, Angus Laverty, Patrick Lonergan, Sheelagh Malin, Monica McInerney, Ger McNaughton, Anne McQuillan, Annique Menninga, Liz Morrin, Pat Moylan, Liz Nugent, Ronan Nulty, Lisney, Siobhan O'Beirne, Tom O'Connor Consultant, Siobhan O'Leary, Muiris O'Reilly, Andrew and Delyth Parkes, Margaret Rogers, David & Veronica Rowe, Judy Regan, Roisin, Jennifer Russell, Eileen Ryan, Coleen Savage, Brian Singleton, William J. Smith, and Mary Stephenson.Thank you also to all those who do not wish to be credited.

fishamble.com

facebook.com/fishamble

twitter.com/fishamble

Acknowledgements

Thanks to the following for their help with this production:
David Parnell, Liz Meaney, Bea Kelleher, Elaine Connolly,
Hannah Gordis, and all at the Arts Council; Ray Yeates,
Sinéad Connolly, and all at Dublin City Council Arts Office;
Sharon Barry, Ciaran Walsh, Valerie Behan, and all at
Culture Ireland; Ronan Nulty, James Kelleher, Karen
Muckian, and all at Publicis Dublin; all at 3 Great Denmark
Street; Fionnuala O'Doherty and family; all those who have
helped since this publication went to print.

Fishamble: The New Play Company presents

Heaven

By Eugene O'Brien

Cast

Mal	**Andrew Bennett**
Mairead	**Janet Moran**

Creative Team

Director	Jim Culleton
Set Designer	Zia Bergin-Holly
Costume Designer	Saileóg O'Halloran
Lighting Designer	Sinead McKenna
Composer & Sound Designer	Carl Kennedy
Dramaturg	Gavin Kostick

Production Team

Producer	Eva Scanlan
Production Manager	Eoin Kilkenny
Associate Producer	Cally Shine
Stage Manager	Steph Ryan
Assistant Stage Manager	Laura Murphy
Assistant Production Manager	Daire Ó Muirí
Chief LX	Síofra Nic Liam
Production Coordinator	Ronan Carey
Marketing	Dafni Zarkadi and Freya Gillespie
PR	O'Doherty Communications
Set Construction	Andrew Clancy
Cover Artwork by	Leo Byrne and Publicis Dublin
Filmed by	Media Coop

The production runs for approximately 90 minutes, with no interval.

Heaven was first produced by Fishamble: The New Play Company, in the Dublin Theatre Festival 2022, at Draíocht and Pavilion Theatre, then toured nationally to Hawk's Well Sligo, Watergate Kilkenny, Everyman Cork, Theatre Royal Waterford, Town Hall Theatre Galway and Belltable Limerick. It transferred to 59E59 Theaters in New York, as part of Origin's 1st Irish Festival in January 2023, and was streamed online.

MA students April Kautner and Sally Stevens observed rehearsals as part of Fishamble's role as theatre company-in-association at UCD. Students from the Lir – Toni Bailey, Sophie Cassidy, and Fibs Porto – took part in design placements.

Fishamble dedicated this production to the memory of Vincent O'Doherty, who was a great friend to the company, and member of the board from 2003 until 2021.

Biographies

Eugene O'Brien wrote the play *Eden*, which debuted at the Peacock Theatre in 2001 and transferred to the Abbey stage later that year and then on to the Arts Theatre in London's West End in 2002. It has been translated into Romanian, Italian, Catalan, Dutch and German. *Eden* received the *Irish Times* Theatre Award, the Stewart Parker Trust Award and the Rooney Prize for Literature. Eugene adapted the play for screen and film, directed by Declan Recks, and played many festivals around the world including Edinburgh Fringe Festival and New York's Tribeca Festival, at which Eileen Walsh won best actress.

Eugene also wrote *Pure Mule*, a six-part series for RTÉ, winner of five IFTA awards and a two-part follow up to *Pure Mule – The Last Weekend*. Other work includes *The Nest*, *Sloth* and *Numb* (nominated for a Zebbie Award) all for RTÉ radio drama and an adaptation of Roddy Doyle's *Barrytown Trilogy* for BBC radio drama.

Other theatre work includes Savoy, produced in the Peacock Theatre, and *The Good House of Happiness* and *Eliza's Adventures in the Uncanny Valley*, both in collaboration with Pan Pan Theatre company.

Other work includes film comedy *The Flag*, starring Pat Shortt, and co-writing credits on the films *The Food Guide to Love* and the Irish Famine drama *Black 47*. Eugene's forthcoming work includes *Tarrac*, a Cine4 Irish-language feature film that debuted at this year's Galway Film Fleadh, *Mespil in the Dark*, a web series and forthcoming theatre show with Pan Pan Theatre, and a novel, *Going Back*, to be published by Gill in September.

Jim Culleton is the Artistic Director of Fishamble: The New Play Company, for which he has directed productions on tour throughout Ireland, UK, Europe, Australia, New Zealand, Canada and the US. His productions for Fishamble have won Olivier, *The Stage*, *Scotsman* Fringe First and *Irish Times* Best Director awards.

Jim has also directed for the Abbey, the Gaiety, the Belgrade, 7:84 Scotland, Project, Amharclann de hÍde, Tinderbox, Passion Machine, the Ark, Second Age, Dundee Rep, CoisCéim/Crash Ensemble/GIAF, Frontline Defenders, Amnesty International, Little Museum of Dublin, Fighting Words, Soho Theatre, Scripts Festival and Baptiste Programme. He has directed audio plays for Audible, BBC, RTÉ Radio 1 and RTÉ lyric fm. He has directed for Vessel and APA (Australia), TNL (Canada), Solas Nua, Mosai and Kennedy Center (Washington, DC), Odyssey (LA), Origin, Irish Arts Center, New Dramatists, and 59E59 (Off-Broadway), as well as for Trafalgar Theatre Productions on the West End, and IAC/Symphony Space on Broadway. Jim has taught for NYU, NUI, GSA, Uversity, the Lir, Villanova, Notre Dame, UM, UMD, JNU and TCD.

Andrew Bennett's previous work includes *She Was Wearing* (Fishamble), *Big Bad Woolf, Foley, Freefall* (Corn Exchange), *The Rehearsal Playing The Dane, The Seagull, Endgame* (Pan Pan), *Le Roi Lear* (Théâtre National Populaire), *Schöne Neue Welt* (Stadttheater Bonn), *The Marriage of Figaro, Lolita, The House* (Abbey). Film work includes *Garage, The Stag, Black 47* and *An Cailín Ciúin*.

Janet Moran is an actor, playwright and director based in Dublin. Selected theatre work includes *Spinning, Swing* (co-writer) and *Rathmines Road* for Fishamble, *Ulysses, The Plough & The Stars, Juno and the Paycock* (National Theatre, London/Abbey Theatre co-production), *Shibari, Translations, No Romance, The Recruiting Officer, The Cherry Orchard, She Stoops to Conquer, Communion, The Barbaric Comedies, The Well of the Saints* and *The Hostage* all at the Abbey Theatre, *Car Show, Dublin by Lamplight, Everyday, Freefall and Desire under The Elms* for Corn Exchange. Film and television work includes *The Dry, Trivia, Love/Hate, Love is the Drug, T* (RTÉ), *Dublin Oldschool, The Bailout* (TV3), *The Butcher Boy, Breakfast* *on Pluto, Milo, Minim Rest, Bono* and *My Ex, Moll Flanders, Nothing Personal, Volkswagen Joe and Quirke* (BBC). She co-wrote the hit play *Swing* and wrote and directed *A Holy Show*, which sold out at the Dublin and Edinburgh fringe festivals as well as its national tour in spring 2020. She also recently directed *My Romantic History, Virtual Verse* (Verdant Productions), *Looking for América* (Dublin Theatre Festival and Edinburgh Fringe), *Pure Mental* (National Tour).

Zia Bergin-Holly is an award-winning lighting and set designer working internationally in theatre, dance, opera and live music events.

Her stage set and lighting designs include *Embargo* (Fishamble*), Solar Bones* (Rough Magic & Kilkenny Arts Festival), *The Misfits* (Corn Exchange), *User not found* (Dante or Die) and *They Called Her Vivaldi* (Theatre Lovett). She also designed the set for the Olympia Theatre performances of Grace Jones concerts for *Bloodlight and Bami* by Blinder Films. Recent lighting designs include *The Border Game* (Prime Cut and Lyric Theatre Belfast), *Skin Hunter* (Dante Or Die), *Two* (Hull Truck Theatre), *Meat* (Theatre 503), *Flights* (One Duck Theatre), *Promises Promises* (Centrál Színház Budapest), *Top Hat* (Silver Blue Entertainment), *Bread Not Profits* (Gúna Nua), *Apologia* and *The Lion in Winter* (English Theatre Frankfurt).

Saileóg O'Halloran's theatre credits include *Duck Duck Goose*, *The Alternative, GPO 1818* (Fishamble), *The Wakefires* (ANU Productions & Cork Midsummer), *Dances Like a Bomb* (Junk Ensemble), *The Secret Space* (ANU Productions), *To The Lighthouse* (Cork Everyman & Hatch Productions), *The Great Hunger* (Abbey Theatre), *The Fall of the Second Republic* (Abbey Theatre & Corn Exchange), *Danse Macabre* (Macnas 2019), *Beckett's Room* (Dead Centre), *The Bluffer's Guide to Suburbia* (Cork Midsummer & DTF 2019), *The Anvil* (ANU & Manchester International Festival), *The Misfits* (Corn Exchange), *Trial of the Century* (Dublin Fringe 2018), *Macnas 2018, Copperface Jacks the Musical* (Verdant), *The Half of It*

(MOMMO), *The Shitstorm* (Dublin Fringe), *The Seagull* (Corn Exchange) *To Hell In A Handbag* (Show In A Bag/Tiger Dublin Fringe), *Town is Dead* (Peacock Theatre), *Embodied* (Dublin Dance Festival), *Shibboleth* (Peacock Theatre), *Chekhov's First Play* (Dead Centre), *Thirteen* (*Irish Times* Judges' Special Award, ANU Productions) and *Wake* (Chamber Made Opera).

Sinéad McKenna is an internationally renowned designer working across theatre, opera, dance and film. She has won two *Irish Times* Theatre Awards for Best Lighting Design and a Drama Desk nomination for Best Lighting Design for a Musical.

Previous designs for Fishamble include *Maz and Bricks, The Gist of It* and *Invitation to a Journey*.

Her other recent designs include *Walking with Ghosts, Straight to Video* and *The Approach* (Landmark Productions), *Maria Stuarda* (Irish National Opera), *Elsewhere* and *Faith Healer* (Abbey Theatre), *Dēmos* (Liz Roche Company), *Parade* (Théâtre du Châtelet, Paris) and *Angela's Ashes: The Musical* (Bord Gáis/Tour).

She has designed for many notable companies including the Gate Theatre, West Yorkshire Playhouse, Donmar Warehouse, Cork Opera House, Lyric Theatre Belfast, Rough Magic, CoisCeim, Gúna Nua, Decadent, Gare Saint Lazare, Corn Exchange, THISISPOPBABY, Siren, Second Age, Performance Corporation and Semper Fi.

Carl Kennedy has worked on numerous theatre productions, working with venues and companies including Fishamble: The New Play Company, The Gaiety, The Abbey, The Gate, Rough Magic, Landmark, Decadent, The Lyric Theatre, Theatre Lovett, ANU Productions, HOME Manchester, Prime Cut Productions, HotForTheatre, Speckintime, Guna Nua and Peer to Peer among others. He has been nominated three times for the *Irish Times* Theatre Award for Best Sound Design. He also composes music and sound design for radio, TV and video games. He was composer and sound designer *for Mr Wall* on RTÉJr which was shortlisted for an IMRO Radio Award in the 2018 drama category. Game titles include *Curious George, Curious about Shapes and Colors, Jelly Jumble, Too Many Teddies, Dino Dog* and *Leonardo and His Cat*. TV credits include sound design for *16 Letters* (Independent Pictures/RTÉ) and SFX editing and foley recording for *Centenary* (RTÉ).

Eoin Kilkenny has toured across Ireland and the world with theatre productions from Landmark Productions, Rough Magic Theatre Company, Fishamble: The New Play Company, CoisCéim Dance, Abbey Theatre and many more. He has worked at some of the best festivals at the Traverse Theatre, Edinburgh during the Festival Fringe, Galway international Arts Festival, Melbourne International Arts Festival, Dublin Fringe Festival and London international Festival of Theatre. He trained as a production manager with the Rough Magic SEEDs programme, working on their productions in Dublin, Belfast and New York. He is a product of UCD Dramsoc and has completed an MA in Producing at The Royal Central School of Speech and Drama.

Steph Ryan has worked in theatre for many years and with many companies including CoisCéim, Rough Magic, Abbey/ Peacock Theatres, OTC and INO to name a few. Work with Fishamble includes *Handel's Crossing, The End of the Road, Noah and the Tower Flower, Spinning, Little Thing Big Thing, Invitation to a Journey* (a co-production with CoisCéim, Crash Ensemble and GIAF), *Mainstream, Rathmines Road, On Blueberry Hill, Embargo, Duck Duck Goose* and Pat Kinevane's *Forgotten, Silent, Underneath and Before*. She is delighted to be back working with Fishamble on *Heaven*.

Laura Murphy graduated from University College Cork with her degree in Drama and Theatre Studies, and worked as a technician and tutor in Granary Theatre, UCC and in Solstice Arts Centre, Navan. She then joined Draíocht,

Blanchardstown as Technical Stage Manager. She is now a freelance stage manager and technician with credits including *Levin & Levin* and *Miss Happiness, Miss Flower* for Broken Crow, *Violet Gibson* for Noggin Theatre, *The Body Brothers* at ESB Scienceblast, *Tradoodle Festival* and *Wunderground* for Ceol Connected, *Alice and the Wolf* and *Swansong* for Barnstorm. She recently joined Fishamble as Venue Technical Manager for their production of *Outrage* at The Pumphouse, Dublin Port.

Eva Scanlan is the Executive Director at Fishamble: The New Play Company. Current and recent producing work includes *Outrage* by Deirdre Kinahan, *The Treaty* by Colin Murphy and *Embargo* by Deirdre Kinahan, both as part of the Decade of Centenaries, *The Alternative* by Michael Patrick and Oisín Kearney, *On Blueberry Hill* by Sebastian Barry on the West End, Off-Broadway and on Irish and international tour, Fishamble's award-winning plays by Pat Kinevane *Before, Silent, Underneath* and *Forgotten* on tour in Ireland and internationally, *The Humours of Bandon* by Margaret McAuliffe, *Maz and Bricks* by Eva O'Connor, *Inside the GPO* by Colin Murphy, *Tiny Plays for Ireland and America* at the Kennedy Centre in Washington, DC, and the Irish Arts Centre in New York; and *Swing* by Steve Blount, Peter Daly, Gavin Kostick and Janet Moran on tour in Ireland, the UK and Australia. Eva produces *The 24 Hour Plays: Dublin* at the Abbey Theatre in Ireland (2012–present), in association with the 24 Hour Play Company, New York as a fundraiser for Dublin Youth Theatre. She has worked on *The 24 Hour Plays* on Broadway and *The 24 Hour Musicals* at the Gramercy Theatre in New York. Previously, she was Producer of terraNOVA Collective in New York (2012–15), where she produced *Underland* by Ally Collier; *terraNOVA Rx: Four Plays in Rep* at IRT Theater; the soloNOVA Arts Festival; the Groundworks New Play Series; *Woman of Leisure and Panic* (FringeNYC), *P.S. Jones and the Frozen City* by Rob Askins, among other projects. She has worked on events and conferences at the New School, the Park Avenue Armory and Madison Square Garden.

Cally Shine has worked across the United States as an actor, teaching artist, company manager and creative producer. Born and raised in Seattle, WA, she holds a BA in Theatre and a Minor in Irish Studies from the University of Montana and a Graduate Diploma in Cultural Policy and Arts Management from University College Dublin. When not working with Fishamble, Cally is an Assistant Producer at Once Off Productions.

Gavin Kostick works with new writers for theatre through a variety of courses, script development workshops and award-winning schemes as Literary Manager at Fishamble. Gavin is also an award-winning playwright. His works have been produced nationally and internationally. Favourite works for Fishamble include *The Ash Fire*, *The Flesh Addict* and *The End of The Road*. Works for other companies include *This is What We Sang* for Kabosh, *Fight Night*, *The Games People Play* and *At the Ford* for RISE Productions and *Gym Swim Party* with Danielle Galligan in co-production with The O'Reilly Theatre. He wrote the libretto for the opera *The Alma Fetish* composed by Raymond Deane, performed at the National Concert Hall. As a performer he performed *Joseph Conrad's Heart of Darkness: Complete*, a six-hour show for Absolut Fringe, Dublin Theatre Festival and The London Festival of Literature at the Southbank. He has recently completed a new version of *The Odyssey*, supported by Kilkenny Arts Festival.

Heaven

Characters

Mairead, *woman in her fifties, married to Mal*
Mal, *man in his fifties, married to Mairead*

Setting

A town in the midlands of Ireland

Time

The present

Mairead I told a lie earlier today. The sister asked what it was like to be home. I said great.

The sister, Laura, then took it upon herself to drive me around the town, a tour, bring me up to date like. I mean, yeah . . . I mean the Dublin road side, you have the three-headed monster – Tesco, Aldi and Lidl – but there is some local business too – Tommy's tyre firm, Moran's Petrol station, Glennan's butchers. Then up onto the square. That's where the rot sets in. Fuck all around it really. No cinema. That's gone twenty-four years. Nothing ever replaced it, and then across the way there is the boarded-up old Tesco. An eyesore. Twenty years since . . . I mean . . . and still no . . . talk of hotels and art centres and Bord na Móna museums but nothing yet. And then further on you have two chemists, a few tattoo parlours, vape and charity shops. That's your lot on the main street and then we swung left, a road opposite the canal bank, down into the vacant office and shop buildings of desolation row and then the fucking piece de resistance; the skeleton of Boylan's folly. The hotel and cinema and shopping centre that never happened. The monument to the madness. The stagnant pools of shite water under the abandoned structure. Boylan, the living embodiment of the tiger years. Him and the wife acted like the bogs' answer to Posh and Becks. He was a councillor. He borrowed crazy money. Owed everyone. When the crash came, there was even talk of these fuckin' Russian gangsters coming after him. Swear to God.

And then we did a full circle back up the town. Saw a family of Chinese and some Poles crossin' the road, nothing agin them now but Laura says that they stay at home to drink. They don't spend in the town, they shell out the few shillings in Lidl or Tesco but that's it. The money is being sent home, which is fine but it's fuck all use to here, to this place. Anyways we're back for Laura's wedding. She finally landed herself a fella. Beano Byrne. A good ten years on her, like he's my age. Was in the home economics class with us. Was caught pissing into a bottle during a detention. Family is a bit, you know . . . I've warned Mal about them. They're grand but a bit out there, up front, don't give a fuck what I do or say to your face kinda people, which I kinda like but a lot don't. Mal will not like this. Mal likes manners and politeness and calm and routine and there's nothing wrong with that, especially after the stents were put in two years ago. Mal is the old man. The hubby. The jockey, once upon a time, Oh yeah, but now the comfortable shoe. The rock. The Mal from the county of Limerick. I'm down there twenty year now ever since we got hitched. In the city. By Jaysus it's improved. Used to be some kip. The city of love I'd joke if you can avoid getting stabbed. I speak my mind and as I say Mal is never happy in his nappy about that but sure he's given up long since trying to . . . ye know . . . that's one good thing about Mal. He never tried to change me.

Our daughter Siobhan was supposed to come with us but she was called into work at the last minute into the hospital, or so she says. She's a Junior Nurse. She's only nineteen but has just moved into an apartment with Wayne, a fierce dull creature who works for his father in a print business. I haven't been to the place yet. Mal has, says it's grand. She's so young like to be shacking up with someone. But it's her life. We rarely talk so, it's . . . ah look it, I mean we don't really, ah look it, the bottom line is that we just don't fucking get on. Same flesh and blood but just cut from different cloth. It happens. We make the effort. We are civil, full stop, Okay . . . Anyways I'm out the night before the wedding. Mal is not. He's been off the drink since the stents and is watchin' the *Late Late* in our room in Bridgie Coyne's B and B as my folks are brown bread so I have no one in the town bar the sister and her place is full with a cousin of Beano's and his partner home from Australia. Mal is happy above in the B and B with Tubridy but I wouldn't be. I'm headin' to Davy's, see if anyone is around. Heard he refused a Traveller and got a beatin' for his trouble. Poor ol' Davy. That's where we used go when we were young, then to Macs, or Club 21 as it's known now apparently. Plenty of Persian rugs on the

go there now if you want them. We saw the solicitor's son,
coming out of the centra earlier on. Laura told me that he is
addicted to heroin. Jaysus, a respectable middle-Ireland lad
doin' the whole fuckin' druggie thing! What chance has
anyone else got?

Anyways into Davy's and a pane of glass in the front window
is still smashed from the night of the Travellers. I see Davy's
bruised face behind the bar. I look to him and he has no idea
who I am. I order a pint of lager with a – 'Howye Davy, long
time no see', and then it clicks and he smiles – 'Mairead,
didn't know ye, long time.' 'Too long.' 'Good woman.' I offer
money but Davy waves it away – 'Nice to see ye.' 'Sorry to
hear about' – Davy's face stiffens – 'Ah sure,' and he reaches
for glasses to go filling other pints and I take a gander
around but I don't really know anyone. There's a few that
nod and say hello but none that I've ever knocked round
with. I hear Hulk Hogan singing in the bar. An amazingly
powerful voice totally off key cos of years of drink and I
think of Siobhan and our last fucking awful phone call and
how much I dislike her and it makes me sad. To actively
dislike your own flesh and blood, and then I spots him.
Large as life and twice as ugly, coming in from the smoking
area, and he's not lookin' bad. The years have been kind
although he used to abuse himself shockin', and pound to a
penny still does. He settles himself at the far counter, talkin'
to some other lad I don't know. He doesn't see me. I take
him in. The bould Breffni Grehan. No-holds-barred full-on
first love straight out of the heart and the groin and feeling
like I couldn't fucking live without him. Twenty I was. At war
with everyone but him. Breffni. And like that he locks eyes
with me. His face breaks into a grin. He gives me the wink.
The same one he gave me in Macs night club thirty years
before and then out onto the town hall steps for the first kiss
and then nights after that of drinkin' and smokin' weed,
which I'd never really done before and ridin' the nights
away in his back room. Jaysus, yeah. He picks up his glass
and he sidles over to me. 'How goes it?' As if he'd just seen

me yesterday as opposed to the years it's been. He has a
slight American twang at the end of the sentences that come
out of his gob, on account of him being in Boston for twenty
years and then when his marriage broke up he moved home
and took up residence in Kells with some Polish one, Ida.
But Ida gave him the old heave ho so he was on the tod now.
There's a new melancholy about Breffni that I like. He
describes the lonely walks in the evening, the long sleepless
nights. I mean he's laying it on a bit for my benefit but the
ol' Breff always had a way with words. I ask why is he home,
back at the scene of his original crimes and he says that's he's
here for the wedding and I remember of course that he used
to pal round with Beano at school and that Beano always
kinda treated Breffni like a super hero! Breffni dared to do
the thing that no one else would. He liked to see himself as a
kind of outlaw. He had a *Mad Max* poster up in his room and
he listened to Nick Cave who I didn't like at the time,
thought he was weird, I was more your straightforward
Whitney girl back then. But anyways Breffni is staring into
me now. The old brown eyes. He had a way of doing that.
Like you were all he was interested in. I could never resist it
even though I knew it was a well-rehearsed ploy to wear ye
down when ye'd sworn that you were never gonna lay a
finger on him again, but you would. And here he is now, at
the same craic and he buys me a drink and there is a silence.
He asks about me. I give up very little. Just bare facts. Mal,
Siobhan. Moving to Limerick. My job. Social worker. He is
pleased that I did something with me self. I say that I got
good practice puttin' up with hopeless cases like him. He
laughs. Another silence before we hear the Hulk Hogan
launching into a song from *Cats*!

I look over at Davy and comment on the Traveller incident.
Breffni bristles at this. He thinks Davy is prejudiced and like
all middle-Ireland respectable folk he bans Travellers first
and asks questions later. 'He should have served them. That
was infringing on their human rights.' Breffni was always a
bit of a right-on dude, talking about American foreign policy

and the Sandinistas in school. He might as well have been talking about Kid Creole and the fuckin' Coconuts for all the sense it made to us! Anyways I say but was that any reason for to give poor Davy a dig. 'No . . . but if you are undermined and oppressed for years an inter-generational anger gets passed down . . . Sometimes it explodes!' Breffni always liked to sound like a lad who went to college, though in fairness he had always been a great reader. I want to get pissed now. I feel like it. I haven't been pissed in ages, not since me and Mal went to Dublin for a few nights on the train and I got locked on wine and Mal had to carry me home and he was vexed all the next day. Dog's abuse I'd say he took. The ol' monster can come out of its box sometimes when I have the few drinks. Mal gets the brunt of it. I ask Breffni does he have any kids and he shakes his head. I have a flash of us fucking in the back room. He always made me come, well the most of the time. One night as Mad Max looked down on us he came and whatever happened, faulty Johnny whatever, two weeks later my period was late and I did a test and what do ye know. Up the duff. I ask him does he remember Birmingham. He nods his head – 'Never forget it'. The evening Ryanair. The people in the B and B – 'I presume you're going to the clinic, we'll call you a taxi'. We went in and it was whipped out. Breffni waited in the waiting room with all the other dads who would not be dads. All ages. All types. We went and had coffee afterwards in BHS and flew home. Breffni wonders what kind of da he might have been. He admits to me that if I had wanted the child in any way he would have stood by me. He kind of regrets it. I say that I don't. He looks a bit hurt but I say nothing. This new less cocksure full of shite Breffni is a better version. But to be really honest I do wonder what kind of child they might have been. The one disposed of in that clinic in Birmingham. Like if it had been a girl would I have gotten on better with her than I do the one I did push out.

Anyways Hulk Hogan is now past it and stumbling along
bumping into people. He spots Breffni – 'Be lord lamb a
Jaysus, fuckin' Breffni Grehan', and launches into Whitney's
– 'I Will Always Love You'. Hulk insists on buying us
whiskeys and pints and the night starts to swirl and Breffni
and me are outside smoking. I haven't pulled on a fag for
years and before I know what's happening we're kissing.
Tongues and the smell of him and the past comes back at me
like a fuckin' train and that real desire for him. Jesus Christ!
Poor Mal back in the B and B and I stop and try to leave but
Breffni pulls me and I push him and he says sorry and how
he'll see me tomorrow and I walk on. Get away. Go on up
the town but I keep seeing his room. The *Mad Max* poster.
His small little bed. My head pushed against the wall, him on
top of me, and me lost, gone from the gate. Me and Breffni,
always so fuckin' good that way . . . you know . . .

I'll get back now to the B and B and warm bed and Mal's
little snore and he'll curl up around me and place his hand
on my back and I'll conk out. Away with the fairies, to a place
where Mairead is okay in herself because she knows that the
fifty years spent on the planet is about to amount to
something. It is all leading to something. Surely it has to be.
Surely . . . It . . . has . . . to . . . Be . . . Leading . . . to . . .
Some . . . where!

Mal   I walk up to Jesus. He looks down on me. I rise my
hands up and touch his chest and I can feel the sweat and
blood and I cry and somehow I'm able to lift him down, off
the cross. His hands and arms encircle me. He looks into my
eyes. I look into his. The most beautiful thing that I have
ever seen. I have an erection. He reaches down and takes
hold of me and he starts to . . . I close my eyes and I'm free,
in my head, completely free and I cry out and . . . and . . .

I refocus now away from the crucifix on the wall of Coyne's
B and B, and the recurring fantasy I used have as an altar
boy. There was a lot of time to fill at the many Masses that I
served at so . . . I loved the smell of the Benediction and

Easter was my favourite feast day when it all came together
and the priest was real good at home. Someone to really look
up to. He wasn't one of them other ones. Home was in
Ballymurphy in Limerick. Rural. A farm. I settle back into
this world where John Coyne seems to feel that it is his
mission to make sure that I, a visitor, know how much the
town is making a slow but sure recovery. He drones on to me
about the green shoots and he bemoans the begrudgers.
'What about the doers. Ye don't hear about them,' I nod and
make positive noises as I finish off the fry. Shouldn't really be
eating dead pig since the stents but every now and again it's
okay. I make my escape up the stairs to the back room that
we are in. Herself is still asleep. Dead to the world. She must
have got in late enough because I didn't hear a hapennth
from her. She was out in the pub. I don't drink. Anymore.
On account of the heart thing a few years ago and . . . well
. . . I found it tough at first but you know, I don't miss a lot
about it. The hangover and recrimination and sense of . . .
well . . . self-flagellation for want of a better word. So I stayed
in with Tubridy until it was time to switch over to this show
that I sometimes watch. It's a thing I'd never admit to
watching and would never dream of looking at if Mairead
was with me. It's a mad show, you know, Channel Four,
where one person chooses from five people to go on a date
but the twist is that their naked bodies are revealed
gradually. First their down below, then the chest or breasts
like and then the face. I love to see who they choose and who
I'd choose. Like which woman would I . . . and then
gradually I started to just want to see the men. It's ridiculous
but it's . . . it's . . . is it my age? It's taking over. Every living
moment. Thinking of Jesus. Feeling anxiety shoot up my
arms. A shortness of breath. I think of my heart and that it
might burst. I have to close my eyes and inhale through the
nose and exhale through the mouth like the nurse showed
me. Calm . . . Calm . . . Okay . . . Okay.

I'll let her sleep on for another few minutes but then I'd
better rouse her. I wonder what way she was last night. She

can get quite inebriated sometimes and has a habit of talking
to herself as if I'm not there, and sometimes she says things
that I definitely shouldn't be hearing. Very personal remarks
about me and Siobhan. They really don't get on. We do. Me
and Mairead always got on. We are the best of pals. But
Siobhan and her are so alike but their world view is so totally
opposed. It frustrates them. This distance. They make an
effort. Things can float along grand but the effort takes it out
of them and sometimes they just can't keep it up and the
Sunday dinners are suddenly full of tension and cross talk. A
battle. Me in the middle like a limp hapless Kofi Annan.
Head down until one of them leaves. It has gotten worse
than that, suffering ducks, I mean to say, blows, like, whacks,
across the face. Siobhan stunned and by the jeanny she hits
back. Christ Almighty tonight but I had to get into the
middle of them. I was kinda relieved when Siobhan moved
out to live with Wayne, a couple of months ago now. I miss
her a whole heap and I talk to her. But Mairead and herself.
Just a lost cause. That's the reality of it.

But me and Mairead don't hit each other. We rub along. We
suit. We found something. She is really very bright. Sharp.
With it. The type of person who could of gone to college
straight off if that had been encouraged. But in their house
it was not the type of thing to be . . . It wasn't on the agenda.
It was all, do the leaving, travel maybe for two years, get a
job ye hate, marry someone ye fell over at the local disco and
boom kids and middle age quickly ensues. But Mairead
wasn't like the rest of the flock. She always did her own
thing. She decided at the age of thirty, the year before I met
her, to latch on to something and train as a social worker,
and she did it, and she's good at it. Now if only I could fix
me self she does laugh, but then you'd lose your edge I say,
and she says that I'd have wanted to know her when she was
younger. She had an edge that fucking drew blood. Excuse
the French. Now she isn't everyone's cup of tea. She doesn't
edit. It all comes out and be the holy fly, it can cause
ructions. She is always taking the piss out of me but it's

affectionate. The day she stops doing that then I know we
are in trouble. She came into my life at a real important
time. A vital intervention. Anyhow I better wake her but the
ol' head is beginning to sink away again. To Jesus. But he's
not on the cross this time. He was over at Laura's house.
Yesterday, where we met Beano and his mad crew. He was a
younger cousin of Beano's. He was Jesus. I couldn't stop
looking. Jesus off the cross and pulling on a cigarette and
wiping blonde hair out of his face and touching his little
goatee and laughing and I was introduced to him. Jesus's
name was Michael, and he was about ten years younger than
Jesus was when he was put up on the cross. I shook his hand.
Electric shock. He had an energy. Something new just out of
reach. He had . . . I have to stop. Heart pumps again. Too
fast and the breath is . . . that's it . . . close the eyes . . .
breathe . . . Calm. Calm . . . Relax.

I open my eyes and see Mairead sitting up in the bed staring
at me. She lets out a yawn and she pops two tablets into her
mouth and washes them down. She needs to be up and at it.
Down at the bride's house. I say that I was just about to wake
her. Mairead grunts. She says that she feels like shite but
manages to shift herself out of the bed and starts to fling on
a few clothes. She doesn't really go into where she was last
night or who she met. Just mutters about a rake a drink in
Davy's and she grabs up her wedding outfit and says, 'See ye
in the church', and she gives me a nice smile before she high
tails it out the door. I get into my suit. I remember the day
we got married. Knowing in a way that she had no real
passion for me. But I didn't care. We had something else. I
told my brother Austin the night before our wedding. I
needed to tell someone. That I knew she wasn't in love with
me like the – 'Can't live without you, tear the clothes off the
back' kinda thing. But that we had something else. A
partnership. A trust. I knew that she was the way I had to go.
There was another way but I just didn't feel it was right for
me. Wouldn't suit the way I wanted to live but I felt I should
try this road before I got married. To get it out of the system.

I didn't tell Austin this bit. I have never told anyone. I
looked up a website and chose him very carefully. I needed
to fancy the person. I needed to experience real desire. So I
chose him. The closest to a Jesus that I could find. I think his
name was Jimmy. He was a North Dub lad, nineteen. We
met in a bar in the Dublin suburbs. Near Lucan. He drank
rum and coke, Captain Morgan's, I drank a gin and tonic.
He had green eyes. Very skinny. I was so nervous I could
hardly speak. He was chatty. 'Relax', he says. I had booked a
room. A Marriot. He stood in front of me and asked what I
wanted and I said that I didn't know. I don't know. He
leaned down and kissed me. He unzipped me. He took me
in his hand. I felt like crying. It was so . . . he said things.
Really nice things but he had been paid to say them. We'd
agreed the money up front. He knelt down but I couldn't
allow that. It was too much. I wasn't able to . . . I couldn't. I
finished then anyway before he had to use his mouth. I
finished very quickly and I was immediately mortified. I ran
to the loo to clean myself off. When I got back he was gone. I
stood in the empty hotel room. I thought about staying the
night seeing as I'd paid for it but I went to meet Mairead to
go to a birthday party of one of her colleagues. I felt a huge
surge of relief come over me when I saw her. I couldn't wait
to be married now and two months later we were.

I'm actually looking forward to today. I liked the sister
whenever I've met her and Beano is rough and ready but a
decent sort. I try to be in the moment more nowadays. Ever
since the stent was put in. I try to breathe and be in the
moment, but it's getting harder. I can't keep my head from,
my whole body from slipping down into this other space,
dimension, whatever the dickens you'd describe it. This
place. With Jesus and that young lad I met yesterday. Down
here where I am me and the world is over there. So far
apart. Which was how I needed it, until a couple of years
ago, lying in the hospital and they said that if I hadn't come
in so quickly I might have died. Ninety per cent blockage in
one ventricle. Woke something back up in me and that night

I dreamt of Jesus, for the first time in ages. Maybe it was the medication but I saw him as clear as day. Walking into the ward. Walking over to me. Bloody face and stigmata and he laid down beside me and took me in his arms and I was never as glad to see anyone.

Mairead   The sister stands before the far east and her groom, the bould Beano Byrne and they say their I dos and she is happy. I can tell. She is beamin' and it makes me feel like cryin' for a moment because God love us where we started out there wasn't that much cause to ever feel good about anything. She got the brunt of it. I stood up to him early on but she took after Ma. Hypnotized into thinking everything was her own fault. I was like him. I was a bully in school. A fierce cunt of a playground terrorist. He kinda admired that in me. That I was a chip off the old block or infected with his cuntism, whatever way you want to describe it. Anyways Laura walks away down the aisle arm in arm with Beano and everyone claps and cheers. The one blessing is that our old man is not above ground to give her away. He left the world ten years ago. Sometimes cancer does cull the right ones! Beano's half of the church already smells of stale drink and they're rarin' for more. I turn to Mal and smile. He touches my arm the way he does. Like he's not sure how to. Like he's going in for to take hold of me arm but then chickens out or feels awkward and then just kinda brushes off it. I catch sight of Breffni. He is sitting near the back in a red jacket. Always the boy who had to stand out. He sees me and nods. I pretend I don't see this. We shuffle on down the aisle after Laura and back to the hotel for the reception, and the speeches and Beano's cousins holding court. There is very few of our side of the family left alive. Thanks be to Jaysus!

Beano's best man is called Declan, but everyone calls him the Hobbit on account of his huge feet. So the Hobbit is in the middle of his speech and it's toe-curlingly awful. The terrible combination of too much drink and a firm belief that you are the funniest man in the room when clearly you have no iota how to tell a yarn with an ounce of wit in it. Instead it's all embarrassing stuff about Beano's past and icky shit that I would shoot him for. Laura pretends to laugh but I know she's ragin' and just wishing that he'd shut up and fuck off back away to Middle Earth! At last the Hobbit pauses as he's just remembered that he forgot to introduce Beano's da. He'd got the order of speeches all wrong, launching into his own first. Wet brain from too much drink last night and the cure earlier today. Anyways little Beano Senior gets up. Seventy-seven and a face drawn thin from the smokes and the drink, his little hand shakes clutching a piece of note paper with scribbles on it. He speaks haltingly and nervously but with great affection about his son. He remembers the time he got a Raleigh chopper off Santa Claus and how Beano Snr had taught him to cycle it. Everything he says is fierce genuine. An antidote to the other fucking egot. We clap warmly. We cheer Beano Snr. I even feel a tear in me eye. Laura's eyes are full of them. So grateful to her dad-in-law that he'd given some proper love and dignity back to the proceedings. But the Hobbit's size twelves are back on the carpet as he launches into some god awful joke and I tune out and take a drink and look to see Breffni slipping away out for a smoke. I place my hand on Mal's arm and I squeeze it. He is surprised. We are not tactile. Not as a rule. He does his awkward touching of my arm thing and listens to the Hobbit's lame joke. I quaff more wine. First one went down real slow, delicate from last night, but now I was over the hump and my system was ready and willing to take in as much lady petrol as I could get down my throat! Flashes of Breffni. His mouth, smell, his hands around my back, trying to get under my shirt. There is applause, cheers, whistles. The Hobbit is over. We all have to stand up and vacate the room while the tables are cleared for the dancing to begin. Breffni is still outside in the smoking area, but I was staying here. Mal likes to dance and I like to dance with him. He can jive and all that, was taught by an Aunt when he was ten and he's never forgotten it. Me and Mal will have a dance and let Breffni smoke fags and spin his yarns outside. We run into

Laura's gang from the meat factory in high spirits and one of them, Joan, a heart as big as her arse, who I knew from long ago, offers me a shot. Sure why not, it's a baby Guinness. Mal gives me a look. I ignore him, knock it back, and laugh at some stupid thing that Joan says – 'the only reason I'd kick him out of bed would be to ride him on the floor!' She's referring to one of Beano's cousins. Some young lad, long hair, beard, like a mini Jesus or something but he looks well in fairness. Mal seems restless. So I take pity on him and promise him a dance as soon as the band sets up. Another man beside us is talking about the immigrants and how we'll be swamped and they get all the houses and everyone's too afraid to say anything and I butt in – 'Fuck that, who are we to be anti-immigrant and we in every country in the world. Irish people are like rats, you're never more than ten feet from one!' Joan laughs. He looks pissed off. Fuck him. I swig me vodka. Mal gives me another look. 'Chill the fuck out Mal. Don't be . . . come on away now and we'll dance' and I grab his arm. The band is up and running. We move onto the floor and spin around to Sweet Caroline!

Mal   She's gone over her limit. I know when it goes over a certain quota the worm can turn and she looks for trouble but the dancing has been a great distraction and we've both enjoyed swinging around to 'Sweet Caroline', 'Walk of Life', 'Wake Me Up Before You Go Go' and 'Hound Dog'. If I can keep her on the floor for the rest of the night it will leave her less time to drink. Avoid a code red. But just as 'Come on Eileen' is starting up she lets go me hand and announces that she needs the jacks. I am kinda glad as I need a little break myself, a bit out of puff. So I sit down, suppin' on me 7UP and taking me ease for a while. A lad plants himself down beside me. A thatch of red hair. Sweat. Loose tie and open collar. I nod to him. I recognize him. One of Beano's cousins. Henny Holohan. He's back from Oz like the rest of them. I introduce myself. He smiles and remarks that Mairead was a gas woman by all accounts. Wild young one.

'Ah yeah so I've heard.' 'Ah sure we all get sense,' he says . . .
'eventually.' His wife Steph wanted to come home and has
decided that they're not going back. Henny thinks it's
madness to stay home. They have work permits and
everything. Steph was working for a grand little salon down
there. He was working as a landscape gardener. He shakes
his head. Steph barrels towards us and she is all blonde
highlights and made up to the nines. She is high as a kite
and talks ninety to the dozen. Henny ignores her. He looks
at her with a kind of disdain. He is determined to fight with
her. You can tell. Determined to take out his frustration on
her because she made him make a decision that he didn't
like. Steph either doesn't realize it or ignores it but she pays
no heed to him and pulls at his hand when 'Dancing Queen'
comes on but there is not a chance of him being led onto the
floor so she gives up and I offer. I am ready for another
dance and there's no sign of Mairead. So I take Steph up
onto the floor and we swing around. 'Ooh, see that girl,
watch that scene, digging the dancing queen'. The song
always takes me right back to my first meeting with Mairead.
It played in the pub while I waited for her to show up. A
blind date. Christ it was the most nerve-wracking week of my
life. Like going for the worst job interview in the world, but
Mairead was brilliant. She did all the talking until I could
relax. I felt so dry and unfunny in her company. But I
enjoyed listening to her. Towards the end of the night I
knew I wanted to see her again. What should I do? How did
it work? Mairead announced that she had no clear idea
either how dating worked. She had never dated in her life
before, she'd just always got locked and fell over someone
and dropped the hand. I laughed and babbled out that I
would like to see her again. She said she would as well. I
seemed like a 'good lad', not like others she'd met. We had
dinner the next Saturday and I knew that I could marry this
woman. I was thirty-four and she was thirty-one and had
made changes in her life. She had sought help. She had
started to look into herself. To see who she really was. She
began to recognize where her destructive urges came from.

Where her need to control came from. She talked about the
bad relationships she had been in. All charmers but men
who sucked the oxygen from the room and left very little for
her. I was bowled over by this courage to change. I needed
someone strong. Someone who would sweep me along.
Keep me here. In this world. Not allow me wander down
below, and I wanted a child. I dearly wanted a child.

'You can dance, you can jive, having the time of your life.'
I'm back in the room, moving around to Abba, but Steph is
more intent on rabbiting on to me. She seems very speedy
talking about her and Henny in the way people talk
nowadays as if the whole world is interested in their
business. She is banging on about the real reason Henny is
so intent on staying in Australia. Steph is convinced that
there was a one who had her eye on Henny at work. 'Big-
titted one, the kind he likes, a hint of the foreign about her,
darker ye know and I know he likes that too. Browsing
history is a great giveaway, ye know what I mean, anyways,
like, she used be textin' him and all this and I ate the
bollocks of him but he maintained that they were just mates
but the thing is, and I'm not a jealous little pathetic little
insecure little, kinda one ye know. I am a woman who knows
her own mind. I just wanted him to want to come home to
Ireland with me but he didn't want to and that hurts me
Mal. It hurts me. Stabs me Mal, it stabs me in my heart. He
wanted to stay in Melbourne with her big fat tits. I knows it.
He's thick now. He won't touch me Mal. He won't lay a
finger on me Mal. Is that fair? I ask ye?'

Now she's clutching my arm. She is definitely on something
that's speeding her up. I have no real experience of these
things but she's on more than Bacardi Breezers. We sit down
then as a slower kinda song comes on, 'The Lady in Red',
and Steph leans into me –'I'm in great form. Flyin'. I'm
being a bit bold Mal. I brought a bit of stuff with me today,
for the craic, for the days that's in it. Haven't taken it in ages
so I've been givin' it a right good go, like it's a celebration
isn't it. It's good, Mal. Have I shocked ye?' I shake my head.

'Have ye ever tried coke, Mal?' I shake my head again. Steph
gets distracted as the bride herself, Laura, is in the vicinity.
My head swims a bit. There is still no sign of Mairead back in
the room. Then I spot Jesus. His beautiful mouth breaks
into a big laugh. I watch the back of his head disappear
through the packed dance floor. I get a notion. Me on coke.
Me speeded up. Me without fear. Me being able to drop
down to the other dimension. The lower one. Mal on coke
could jump down and land and take his place in that
dimension with Jesus. Could he? I smile at Laura as she
passes by and she asks am I having a good day and I say the
best and how I'll want a dance later and she asks where her
sister is and I say I don't know. 'Keep an eye on that one
Mal,' and she laughs and I laugh and she moves on and
Steph is fiddling with her hair and looking over to where
Henny is, laughing with big Joan who is giving out all the
signals. At least that's what it looks like to me but what would
I know. Steph is raging but determined not to seem
bothered. She gets to her feet. She is about to march. I know
she must be going to the jacks to refuel. I find myself on my
feet after her. I find myself walking behind her. Through the
wedding guests, staff coming in with trays of sandwiches for
the afters. Steph spots me behind her and grins. We head
out through the doors of the function room, into the
corridor. I have to say something now or I'll look like a
terrible fool. So I look her in the eye, clear my throat and say
. . . Trying to see myself as some sort of cool dark horse fifty
plus coke snorting fiend and I come out and say it – 'Eh . . .
Steph . . . sorry but like . . . I was just wondering like if it was
cool like . . . I was just wondering if I could score off you?'
She says nothing. Her face freezes. Like she has lost the
power of speech. Then her face creases into laughter. Tears
roll down her cheeks. She can't control herself. It is the
funniest thing she has ever heard. Mal asking to score some
coke off of her. I stand humiliated. I am about to turn and go
when she grabs my arm. 'Sorry Mal. Sorry. It's just the way
ye . . . sorry. Okay, come on.' She nods over to the front
doors of the hotel. She winks and says – 'Folly me!'

We sit in the front seats of their car. A saloon of some sort. It
is parked well away from the front of the hotel. Trees
overhead. It is safe. Because I may be about to leave this
dimension. The one I was born into. Attending the Crescent
and notions of the Jesuits but teaching instead and safe holy
home with Mam and Dad and their honeymoon in Lourdes
and never a cross word and complete faith. To do as they
were told. A nation of obedient children. I found great
comfort too in the Mass, the ritual, the confessions. The last
one I ever did was after the Marriot hotel but I couldn't tell
the priest what had happened with the . . . the hired hand,
so I made up sins like you did when you were a child. I
blathered out harmless stories of being less than Christian
towards my parents blah blah but all I wanted to confess was
that Jesus had . . . that he had been in front of me, that I had
come in front of Jesus. I watch Steph cut the coke into little
lines, like I've only ever seen in the movies. Was I about to
leave this life? This fucking dream world that I float through
and never fully inhabit. Fuuuucckkkk, I should just get out
of the car. Now. Coward. Do it! Coward! That's what you are!
Mal. Mal, who the fuck is Mal. I feel kind of sick at myself. I
could vomit at the thoughts of who I am. I should open the
door. I put my hand over to the handle to get out but I
don't. I stop. I wait. I can hardly breathe. Steph has the euro
note rolled up to her nose and she lowers the head and
hoovers it up. Then she grins and hands me the note. 'Your
go Mal.' She sniffs and smiles and it's too late to turn back
now, so I lower the head and do the same and feel a sharp
sensation in the nasal passage and it's not terribly pleasant
but she urges me to go again so I do, into the other nostril
and it feels kind of numb now in the snoz so I settle back in
the seat and wait for the effect. There will be nothing to hold
me back then. Nothing to stop me from digging deep, to the
underneath, where I will go in search of Jesus.

Mairead   I've been gone ages now. In the smoking area, to
the rear of the hotel. I've stalled the ball on the drink for the
past little while so I am all cooled off and zen-like. The

picture of patience waitin' for this young one to stop bangin'
on to Breffni about how she blogs every week about the way
to live your best life. She is either into Breffni, which would
be unbelievable as she is half his age, or she's on something.
My vote is the latter. There's no one into Breffni here, bar
me of course. I have admitted it to myself. After the wine
and the dance with Mal I sauntered out to the loo and I sat
on the seat for longer than I needed to. I admitted it to
myself. I have never fancied anyone as much as Breffni. We
fitted that way. Some people are just tuned in sex-wise and I
could feel him wanting the same, or at least I thought I did.
It's been so long since . . . It's been five years and a few
months since me and Mal had a go. It was Easter time. Jesus
had just risen from the dead when Mal attempted to do the
same but it didn't last. He lost his . . . ye know, before we
could properly get going. He finished me off as best he
could with his hand and I pretended to . . . Ye know . . . just
to make it stop. He clearly didn't want me anymore that way
anyway and I had long since lost my mojo for Mal so we shut
up shop. I did think about counselling with this woman I
knew, who specialized in tryin' to get long-term marrieds
horny for each other again. This woman advocates role-
playing in the bedroom. Can you imagine Mal role-playing?
I mean, no, I just couldn't put him through it. Let him read
his book about Stalingrad and roll over and go to sleep. So I
haven't been there in a long time and I wanted to be. I felt it
deep in the guts of me that I needed to be . . . And Breffni
was here and Mal couldn't mind so I was going to suggest
something. If I could only get the Millennial Minnie to stop
her incessant shite talk and fuck off. Breffni does it for me.
Good old Breff excuses himself and heads for the loo. He
winks at me and indicates the hotel lounge bar as he's
turning. I leave your one standing about to open her gob
about 'sustainable living' and head through to the bar and sit
on a stool at the counter. I order more wine and a pint for
him. I think about what I am doing. I try to float above
myself and look down and see myself clearly. Out of body
like. I am going to ask my ex lover to sleep with me whilst

my husband, blissfully unaware, jives to the Midnight Blue
wedding band. Has it come to this? All my fifty-plus years on
the planet have been leading to this. Really? I take a good
gulp of wine. A flash of Mal comes into me skull. Tears in his
eyes, crying after he came home from school one day last
year. Some boy had called him a queer or something. Mal
had tried so hard with this disadvantaged lad from the
council flats, for to get his Leavin'. Put his heart and soul
into this lad but the lad had insulted him one day. Mal had
berated him for not working as hard as he had been and the
lad called Mal a queer. Poor Mal, he was so hurt. He doesn't
cry easily. I held him. And soothed him like a child until he
stopped and dried his eyes. He looked to me and said thank
you. 'I am so glad I have you,' he said.

I gulp back more wine and think about giving the whole
thing up when Breffni skips in beside me, whooshes up the
pint and takes a large swallow. He laughs about the young
one in the smoking area, how she'd never shut up, 'eat pray
love shite.' I laugh and shake my head – 'It's all so, me me
me, fuckin' up their own holes . . . Who is she anyway, was
she after a bit of the ol' Breff,' 'Would ye go way,' says he, 'I'd
be arrested.' I palled with her old man Red Ryan long ago.
She's on a quare buzz anyhow. I think there's coke goin'
around. Some of Beano's cousins have a load of it, 'Do you
ever?' I asks him. 'Ah no. Gave that all up. This is enough for
me now.' He nods to his pint. 'Sometimes it's more than
enough.' He shakes his head and sighs and says that Ida, the
ex, didn't drink. 'Not even vodka and she from Poland.
She'd sit sipping a coke and I'd be boozing away. I mean I'd
try to go easy but once I start, ye know . . .'. I nod to him,
racking me head as to how to get around to . . . what? Just
ask him out straight. You're both old enough and ugly
enough. Ask him if he wants to . . . sleep with . . . No, too
formal. Have the ride? No . . . too . . . Too kinda jokey. Do
you want to fuck me? No, you're not in a Jaysus porn. So I
open me mouth, take a leap, trusting that something will

come out. 'Breffni, do you want to go somewhere and you
know . . . the way we used to.'

Breffni sits, kinda stunned. He takes a drink. He looks back
at me. His mouth curls into a shy kind of smile. 'I would love
that. I always thought of us, ye know, it was some wild thing
we had, but it's mad Mairead, your old man in there jivin' to
the music and he seems real decent and' – I interrupt him. I
have to lay it out. 'Mal is my best friend, always will be, but
we don't do anything physical anymore. He doesn't care
Breffni. He feels guilty if anything. Like he wishes someone
would take the burden off of him.' Breffni looks to me, 'Well
he's mad. You still have it all goin' on Mairead.' I shake me
head and let on I think he's messin' but so fuckin' glad that
he said it. I see us now in the room. What room? Where will
we go? 'Where will we go,' I say again, this time out loud.
Breffni pauses. He is suddenly furtive, almost coy, Like it's
real and now he has to actually do something about it. He
says in a real low voice, 'I have a key for the old place.' His
box room flashes into me head. The *Mad Max* poster, the
small single bed. I nod and we finish our drinks in silence.
Nervous now. The deal has been done. We are entering
uncharted waters. Two fifty-year-olds are gonna try to light
each other up like they used to all those years ago. Breffni
gets up off his stool – 'I'll split off. Give it a minute and then
follow me on.' I nod. He heads off. I feel a tingle, an old-
fashioned shoot of – Jesus, is this happening? You better
believe it girl. I give it a few more seconds and then move. I
walk through the lobby of the hotel, on the watch out for
Mal or anyone else I know, but I am able to make a clean
break, out the front door. Into the car park, through the
front gates, along the road towards the town. I text Mal.
I can't not text him. I say that I felt sick and have gone
home. Nearly asleep. Please stay out and enjoy yourself. What
happens if he insists on coming back immediately. What
happens if he arrives into the B and B in an hour and I'm
not there. What happens if we all fuckin' die tomorrow? I
hurry on, past pubs and drunken skins and young ones

roarin' and I near the door of the house. I text that I am
approaching. The door opens. I push. I step in. Before I
know what has hit me Breffni is on me, mouth on my mouth.
He has me pinned to the wall. His late Ma's sacred heart
looking down on us. I kiss him back, by Jaysus it's great to be
kissing someone again. Let's get at it! I pull him down the
hall towards the back of the house. He asks where am I
goin'? He reminds me that it's thirty years since I've been in
the place. It's been done up. There's a bigger en-suite to the
left of the kitchen. He re-directs me in the door of this
absolutely . . . I mean compared to his old pokey cold back
bedroom, it's a fuckin' palace and a big decent double bed
and I pull him down onto it and I yank the red jacket off of
him and we kiss like we've only just discovered it, and that
it's the best thing ever that anyone could ever do! We pull
each other's buttons and zips and straps and he's breathing
heavier than he used to, the thirty more years of smoking
taking its toll, but we're there, in that weird and wonderful
place, we are right there. Me and the bould Breff and our
bodies mightn't be as tight as they once were but by Jaysus
we know the ropes and we go at it now. At it now. What can I
tell ye. I feel like tears. The release of it, and he groans, he is
gone from the gate. I will soon follow him.

Mal   Back inside this good while now and I really am
feeling very little. I mean I am kind of disappointed. I'm
tapping my foot along to 'Rockin' All Over the World' and
watching Steph chat up some man with a huge head and no
chin. Henny looks worse for wear now and is in a cluster of
the cousins and Beano seems to be trying to calm him down.
It could 'all kick off' as they say. I scan the room but there's
no sign of Jesus. Where is Jesus? I take out my phone to
check the time. I see that there is a text from Mairead. She's
gone back to the B and B. Feeling sick. Too much vino even
for her. She'd usually have to be dragged out kicking and
screaming. She'll be like a briar tomorrow, but tomorrow is
tomorrow Mal. Look around. I'm feeling kind of hot. They
start up 'New York New York' and everyone's on the floor

but there's still no sign of Jesus, 'Start spreadin' the news.
I'm leavin' today.' I do feel warm, dry and need a drink so I
go to the bar and order a tonic water, but then before I know
what I've done I ask the barman to give me a gin as well. I
mix them and drink them and it's the nicest drink I've ever
tasted. I sink it. Stents or no stents. I'll be grand. I feel a
creeping surge of, what is it, excitement. It's new. This
feeling. It's . . . where will it end? I order another G and T
and drink it back and there's just something about the room
now. The atmosphere in the room now, like they are all here
in my show. My story. They are all dancing to the beat of my
drum. It's not Laura's day at all. It was all set up for me.
This whole day was set up for Mal. It somehow was all going
to be about me and who I am and I stride through the
dancers and gulp back my gin and tonic. Mairead is not part
of this night. This is Mal's night. It's like it's all leading
towards something. I feel it in my waters. I feel it pumping
around my blood into my heart, my stent, fit as a fiddle,
raring to go. Where is Jesus? Just to talk to him, say a word
or two. Share a moment or two but I can't see him anywhere
and then I'm pulled into the line for Frank Sinatra and
everyone's kicking the legs, 'If I can make it there. I'll make
it anywhere', and I'm thinking about ducking out of it, but
it's like a scrum and then something happens to my left. A
movement. A roar. I look across. The whole room looks
across. Steph's high-pitched string of curses mixes with
Henny shouting about how he will fucking tear this lad's
head off. The man with no chin who Steph had been
chatting up. It's all got out of hand. Henny has boiled over.
He has the chap by the throat and he is threatening to
squeeze the fucking life out of him. Steph is trying to pull
him off. Others rush in and try and calm the situation but
Henny will not let go. I find myself moving forward with one
hand raised in the air, like I am about to wave a white
handkerchief. Don't shoot. Please. I am rounding on Henny
like he will listen to me and no one else, like I have the
power to calm the beast, a Doctor Dolittle, I can talk to the
animals and Henny squares up to me but I have no fear and

I look him straight in the eye. 'Let it go Henny. You're a
bigger man then this,' and he lets go of your man's throat
and I shake my head and smile and he smiles, and Steph is
livid and storms off and Henny puts his arm around me and
we move off away from the crowd. Sinatra finishes off but it's
been kind of ruined and Laura and Beano look real thick
and me and Henny get outside the room and Henny leans
into me and says he's knows where there'll be loads of craic
and no shite and no Steph. He wants Mal, his new best pal,
to come with him, back to the cousin's room. Room 131.
Henny and me away down the corridor and before I know it
he is rapping on the door of 131 and it opens. Jesus stands
in front of us with a bottle of beer and what looks like a joint
in his mouth. 'Hiya men,' says Jesus. And I know that he is
the most beautiful thing that I ever seen. Through him, with
him, in him, in the unity of the Holy Spirit. All glory and
honour are yours Almighty Father. For ever and ever. And
we file past Jesus and into the room.

Mairead   It's a kind of pastel-coloured wallpaper above the
bed and a white ceiling. I look up. Breffni lies beside me. I
know he's dying for a smoke so I kick him with my foot and
say, 'Go on out and have a fag.' He grins and leaps up naked.
Funny how everyone gets a bit shy when the ridin' is done.
He kind of hides his bollocks with his hand until the boxers
are pulled on. I lean up to him and kiss his face. 'Thanks
Breff,' that was, ye know, thanks like . . . for the pleasure of
it.' He is taken aback. He nods, 'Ah yeah, thank you.' He
wants to say more but hesitates and then decides to retreat
from the room. I lie there. I stroke my belly, my breasts. I
think of other lovers. Jaysus there was a fair few in my
twenties. Jim, Colm, Dano, Jacko, Dave, Mike, Charlie who
along with Breffni was the best in the bed, and then there
was others, one-nighters. A guard from Borrisokane who
had the biggest . . . I ever saw. But now here I am. I think
about what has just happened, here in this bed, with the
bould Breff. Things he did. Things I did. Jaysus. Not bad for
ol' ones. FFF . . . Fine for fifty. I got lost in moments, in a

place far away from Mairead and her life and her planet. It
felt good to be travelling, into deep space. My fifty years
been leading to . . . what? The truth is out there! My head
swims with possibility and a need for . . . What? Mairead.
Who are you? I am a mother. I think of Siobhan in some
hospital corridor and her apartment with the dopey fella
and she so young really to have committed so early to him
and the resentment she has for what she blames me for and
our lack of being able to connect, and I suddenly feel tears.
It's the drink and the sex and now her, Siobhan. It makes
me cry. Breffni appears back in the room. Alarmed when he
sees my tears. Oh no. Crazy emotional woman alert! But I
grin and say. 'It's okay, get into the bed.' And Breffni climbs
back in under the duvet and he looks at me. All soulful like,
and he starts to speak, very hesitantly at first. About us. He
really wants to talk about us. Oh fuck. He wants to talk about
the future and what are we both at and how he has never
forgotten me and this just proves it. That the universe has
spoken. We are meant to be together. He is certain of this.
He stops. I rub his inner thigh, feel if there is any action just
beyond it that might stop his talking but he puts his hand on
mine and lifts it out. He says – 'Mairead. I love ye. I want
you to come away with me. I have money saved. I have my
eye on a cottage in Kerry. Out near the Atlantic. Where we
could live. We could really live properly Mairead. Not just go
through the motions.' I am so surprised. I laugh. I mean, I
look at him. Is he being serious? He is. He says that he's
thinking of giving up the drink. He's been reading a lot
about Buddhism. A new way to live but he needs me with
him. There is silence now. I look back at the white ceiling. I
say, 'So when did this grand plan strike ye? Just now outside
havin' your smoke?' 'No,' he says, 'I was thinkin' about it
ever since I got Beano's invitation. I knew you'd be here. I
knew I might have a chance to put it to you. I prayed that
we'd still feel the same way about each other.' 'How do ye
know how I feel?' I shoot back to him. 'I don't,' – he says, in
fairness. Like he has laid it all out there without any
guarantee. I look at him. I kiss his lips. I draw back from

him. I try and go there. Me and the Breff by the sea and our
little house and him praying to a Buddha and me all healthy
and happy and we ride every day or want to and I suddenly
feel a turn in me stomach. A turn the right way. A turn that
makes me feel like this could be, maybe, a monu-fuckin'-
mental night of my life. And he kisses me. He knows I will
have to go back to Mal tonight, but he will be waiting for me
in the square in the morning. He will drive off at nine
whether I turn up or not. He seems so certain. He believes
in destiny he says. I get up and lean down to find me clothes.
I dress in silence. He watches me. He says again that he loves
me. I lean back and kiss him. I head off. I don't look back. I
am getting nearer to something. The answer to the question.
Who am I? A woman who leaves her husband very suddenly
for an old lover and heads to a cottage in Kerry? Be the
Jaysus maybe I am. Is this where the fifty plus years of life
has been leading me? Be Jaysus maybe it is.

Mal   I'm sitting on the edge of the bed drinking a bottle of
beer. They have a load of it in the bath with ice. A girl called
Jessica is perched in beside me and she hasn't stopped
talking since we came in. It's some sort of high drama
involving her friends which she is hell bent on telling me. In
fact every single body in the room is hell bent on telling each
other a whole bunch of stuff but nobody is listening. It is a
hotel room full of voices. The Hobbit, his brother Flipper,
Big Joan and of course Jesus, my eyes full of Jesus, his lips
moving and his hand at his beard and pulling back his hair
out of his amazing eyes. Henny slouches on a chair in the
corner. Thick that all the coke is gone. They only have grass
now, and Flipper is trying to roll it and Joan is leaning over
him, but he is more interested in Jessica who is younger and
prettier and has the full makeup on and the eyebrows and
the no skirt and Henny is fixated on her as well. Hobbit is
the drunkest of them all. He is sitting in behind Joan and
making lewd comments about her ample bosom. She gives
shit back to him with as much disdain as she can manage in
her voice, mainly about the fact that he lacks a penis and

how she'd be far too much for him to handle. Joan is far more interested in Flipper, who is still trying to get the joint together, and Jessica's words continue to pour out of her. I nod to let on I'm listening. Then my body gets a little shot of electricity through it. Jesus sits the other side of me on the bed. Jessica is immediately drawn to him. She even shuts her gob for a second. Flipper turns and offers the joint to her. She takes it and lights it and she inhales and blows out smoke and she offers to give Jesus a blow back, which strikes me as being quite alarming. What did it mean? A blow back? Some sort of blow job? Jesus the millennials are so free . . . no guilt . . . But much to my relief I witness what a blow back is. She blows smoke into his mouth essentially and he inhales and it does look intimate but they do it very casually and Jesus smiles and thanks her and she beams at him. Flipper takes the joint and takes a pull and seems to accept defeat in the Jessica stakes. He will settle for Joan now so he offers her a go at the joint and she leans her ample bosom into him to take it. Henny is still very broody lookin'. Eyes boring a hole into Jessica. The Hobbit is up on his giant feet and stumbling over to the bed. He wants to be where the action is. I get up and let him sit down. I retreat to the other armchair. It was getting too much for me, the proxmity to Jesus was too much. He seems a quiet, very self-contained kind of a lad. Happy in his own skin. Everyone else has a lairy, nervous drugged-up energy. A frustration that is on the verge. I think about going. I think about beating a path to the door when Jessica looks over in my direction and holds up the joint. And she says, 'G'wan ye legend, still up partyin' and you an ol' fella, fair fucks to ye. Want some?' I would like some. I haven't smoked since college in Maynooth, and I got paranoid and threw up in the bushes. Jessica keeps the joint held out, 'Well, come on, did ye want some?' and then I can hardly believe what I am seeing. Jesus takes it out of her hand and he steps across to me. He hands me the joint. He sits down on the arm of the chair. I take a pull, feel it harsh at the back of my throat. I cough but I manage to keep it in my lungs. I have another go. I feel the lift, the relax, the drift. Jesus takes it from me and takes a drag. I hope for one crazy second that we will get to do the blow back thing but he passes the joint to Henny who takes an aggressive pull. Joan and Flipper are necking on the other end of the bed. The Hobbit is near conked out. Henny shifts himself over to the bed to sit with Jessica. He is making his move now that Jesus is no longer beside her. She looks across at Jesus with a great yearning but he is beside me. Jesus is looking at me. He is leading me through the wilderness, avoiding regret and fear and keeping me calm. Jesus asks me something. He wants to know what I'd do if I had only one day left on the planet Earth. I can answer this. I don't think, I just say the first thing that comes into my head. I would try and give my students one last useful lesson. To really get through to them. To leave them with something that they would remember for the rest of their lives. 'So what would you say?' Jesus asks me. I hesitate. He gestures towards the room, 'Come on, this is the class room, get up and give it to us.' I stand. I will tell them everything I know. I will stand tall. Jesus wants me to speak. The rest of them ignore me but I don't care, something is flowing through me now. A great power and I am going to own this power. Use it. Speak my truth. Jesus is at my side. So I speak up. I shout. Hey everyone. I want to say something. I want to tell you all something. Flipper and Joan come up for air. Henny and Jessica look over. The Hobbit is flat out on the bed but raises his head. Jesus urges me to keep going so I do. I am so pleased that you were all able to make it today, it has been a pleasure to teach you. I'm sorry but this is my last day. I want to tell you about the shadow. It is something buried deep down in us that we suppress and this causes us to hide. Out of the light, out of our true natures. We are afraid. We are lashed to the mast of duty or who we think we should be and we betray our potential for happiness and really living a life. Jesus looks up at me. I am raised up. I am preaching the sermon from the mount and Jesus is listening. Henny stands. He is being inspired too. He is lifted. My words fill the room. GO OUT FROM THIS PLACE AND BE TRUE

TO YOURSELF. THEN AND ONLY THEN CAN YOU
TAKE YOUR PROPER POSITION IN THE
COMMUNITY OF THE WORLD. GAME B IS COMING.
REACH OUT TO YOUR FELLOW HUMAN BEINGS. A
NEW WAVE IS ON THE WAY! It's like I am speaking in
tongues. Like a great truth is gushing out of me, and Jesus
smiles. He claps. He is applauding me and I am ten foot tall
again. I am flying now, and I reach out for his hand. He
takes it. He lifts my hand above his head, like I am a sports
champion or something. I lean in to Jesus. I want to tell him
how I once dreamed of him and yearned for him to come off
the cross. He opens his lips to say, 'I hear you man. I hear
your truth' and he hugs me. And I put my hand down, onto
his knee and squeeze his knee and I lift my face away and
look into his eyes. Pupils dilating. High, so high. The black
and white film they showed us in school of the Judas kiss in
the garden. Gave me the horn. Judas kissing Jesus in the
garden. So I lean in and I kiss my Jesus on the forehead and
it's a kiss of love not betrayal. I am not Judas. I am Mal. For a
moment time stops. Then he draws back away from me. He
opens his eyes, as if coming out of a dream or just waking
up. I look at his lips. I move my face down. I can feel his
breath. I am about to gently touch his lips with mine when
suddenly Henny has me by the collar and he is shouting at
me, hauling me towards the door, shouting names. 'Queer!'
Henny wants to kill something. He raises his fist. I brace
myself. Jesus intervenes. He grabs Henny's arm and pulls
him back. He insists that everything is cool and to sit back
down with Jessica. He asks Flipper to roll another joint real
quick. Jessica urges Henny to calm down. Jesus pats Henny
on the back, 'Have another beer. Have another smoke. All
will be good dude.' Jesus nods at me. He is taking care of
me, shepherding me, out of the lions' den, out the door of
the hotel room, into the corridor. I want to thank Jesus. I
want to say so much to him, but I don't have the words.
Standing in the hotel corridor, he says that it was real good
to meet me and that he really liked what I said. He grins, ' I
am kinda bi, ye know, but you're a bit old.' I want to say

words but am struck dumb. Then out of nowhere I say . . .
Words start coming out of me. Words I remember from long
ago, '*Auribus teneo Lupum. Aut cum scuto aut in scuto. Disce quasi
semper victurus vive quasi cras moriturus. Aut viam inveniam aut
faciam. Igne natura renovator integra.*' Jesus smiles and nods.
He likes the Latin. He asks what it means. I say roughly that
I am holding a wolf by the ears and it's do or die. I have to
live as if tomorrow is my last day alive. That I have to find a
way or make one. That through fire nature is reborn. Jesus
likes this. He leans forward very slowly and kisses my lips,
very softly, with great affection and then he goes back inside.
I am alone. I am floating on air. I am feeling complete and
utter rapture. I am away. I am never turning back from this
moment. I have disappeared. Underneath. I am staying
here. Away from the other place. The surface world. I have
been there too long. It's time for me to stay under here.
Forever. Where I belong. Where I can really live. Jesus grant
me the courage to do so.

Mairead   I wake to see Mal beside me. He is snoring lightly.
He looks content the way he always does when he is
sleeping. I try to get out of bed but find that I can't move my
arms or legs and Mal's eyes suddenly open wide and he
screams. A full-throated hysterical scream that sends the
fuckin' fright of Christ straight through me and I wake up
with a jolt. Smack bang back to this world! I am back in the
land of the living, in Coynes B and B and I rub my eyes and
I look across and think that I must be still dreaming as Mal is
nowhere to be seen. His side of the bed is empty. I am
absolutely amazed. Knock me down with a fucking feather.
It's half seven in the morning and Mal has not slept in his
bed. The dirty stop out. I laugh. What the fuck could have
happened him. No missed calls from him. Jaysus, I hope
he's okay. I start to worry then. Did his heart give way again?
Is Mal lying some where, and then I think – It would save
me having to tell him, that I was leaving him, if he was dead
like. What a cunt I am. Anyway someone would have rang
me if he'd collapsed. No . . . He must have stayed at the

hotel. Very unlike him though. My phone bleeps. I sit up to
reach for it. That will be him. But it's not Mal. It is from
Breffni – Hope to see u later. I love u. What was I doing? I
was moving, at last I was moving, to somewhere else. Stalled
for so long. I had given over my body to Breffni, I mean I
trusted him with it, he could do whatever he fuckin' liked to
me. It was all so good. It would take time for the other, for us
to really get in tune or whatever with our inner selves and
monsters and egos and the whole works but I think we
could. I think. He's open. He's coming towards me. Mal was
always retreating. The Breff will pull up into the square at
nine and wait for me. Jesus, that's in an hour! Where the
fuck is Mal! I need to find him. I give him a call, but again I
just get his business-like 'please leave a message for
Malachy'. I was always on to him to change that thing. Most
people ringing wouldn't know who Malachy was. He is Mal.
Mal. I have to find him. I get up out of the bed. I dress. I'll
have to go looking for him. I stuff the few clothes into me
bag and rush down the stairs and out the front door of the B
and B. I think John Coyne calls after me but I ignore him. I
have to find Mal.

I hurry along. Hungover and dehydrated from last night
but adrenalin is shooting through me system and the
madness of what I am about to do. I come out on the Dublin
road side of the town. Past the three-headed monster, Aldi,
Lidl and Tesco and past Moran's petrol station and Tommy's
Tyre firm and Glennan's Butchers and up onto the square,
my mind racing, I'll be back here at nine to meet Breffni. My
heart pumps and I think of some of what we did in the bed
and I smile and my phone rings. I whip it up but it's not
Mal. And it's not Breffni. It's my daughter. Siobhan. Jesus,
no, of all the . . . I would usually ignore her but decide to
pick up just in case she has heard from Mal, 'Hi . . . Hi
Mam.' 'Yes . . . This is she.' 'Yeah . . . hi . . . Sorry for ringing
so early. Did you have a good night?' 'Yes,' I say and I tell
her that her Father is a right rock and roller and stayed out
all night and she pauses and laughs and says – 'Yeah right.'

She asks about Laura and Beano and apologises again for not being able to make it. Her voice is small or something, there is no edge, there is no air of confrontation or picking a fight or Mam I don't understand you. I say that I'm dying of a hangover and she laughs and adds that sure what are weddings for only to have the few and no hint of recrimination about the drinking because that had often caused problems between us in the past. Me coming in a little bit pissed and getting thick with her and her attitude to me and her slavish devotion to her Da and her little miss even-tempered passive-aggressive act versus my bull in a china shop. I feel I should be the next to speak so I ask about her shift at the hospital and she says it was fine, nothing too out of the ordinary. I feel I should ask after Wayne. So I do and she says that he's okay but that she finds the apartment a bit small and she hesitates and she adds that he is a bit of a creature of habit. I can't help myself, 'That doesn't surprise me. Men like that always are. Old before their time.' Siobhan interrupts me – 'Please Mam I don't need,' I plough on, 'Fuckin' pipe and slippers and . . .', her voice tenses up, 'Please Mam . . . I know what you think of him but . . .', I press on, I want the fight, 'I mean Jesus do you still have sex?' 'Shut up Mam,' 'Does he still want to ride ye like.' 'Shut the fuck up Mam.' 'I mean why you had to move in with him I'll never fuckin' know.' Siobhan suddenly explodes, 'To get away from youuuuu!!!!' I am about to launch a missile right back at her but I hear her crying. Real sobbing and she has not cried in my presence since she was nine or ten no matter how many times I've fought with her. So I stop myself. I bite the lip. I walk on past the closed-down Tesco and on down the main street, past the tattoo parlour and bookies and vape shops and I say, 'Siobhan, come on. What's up with ye?' She clears her throat. She hesitates and then speaks – 'I'm pregnant. I took a test when I got home this morning. He doesn't know. I don't want to tell him. I can't tell anyone. I don't know why I even rang you, cause of the way we do be, but sometimes you just need your Mam.' I hold my breath at this. I feel a surge of

emotion shooting up from deep inside me and I walk on
past desolation row and Boylan's folly in the distance. I keep
on walking and I say to her – 'Do you want to keep it
Siobhan?' She says nothing and I can hear the tears again
and she says that she just doesn't know. She doesn't love
Wayne anymore. She knows that much. I try and stop myself
being pleased over this. I can hear the ten-year-old girl on
the phone and I am the Mam. She just needs her Mam. But
all the bad feeling and resentment caused by our ongoing
battle of wills, is like a chain around me neck, strangling me,
squashing words in me throat. And then she tells me that
she's sorry. For us always fightin' and . . . she knows how
rough it was for me growin' up. That I had a lot of shite to
deal with and she is sorry for not always allowing me that. I
choke now. She was always more adult than I was. She was
always a strong and true little soul. I was a coward. She goes
on, like it's gushing out of her. She thinks she might like to
have the child but is shit scared that it would . . . the thing
inside her might grow up and cause pain . . . the pain that
she's only ever seemed to have caused me. I feel like I have
been kicked in the stomach. All the emotion that I am
holding just bursts out. I just break down. I lose it. I keep
saying sorry. I'm sorry . . . I can't find any other sounds to
make . . . I want to give her comfort. I want to take back the
poison that I've inflicted on her over the years. I want to . . .
but all I can do is cry. Tears streaming down now. I see one
of Beano's cousins staggering down the road with big Joan.
They are both too out of it to see me. Siobhan's little voice
appears in my ear. 'What am I going to do Mam?' All I can
say to her is that that everything will be okay. Everything else
matters for fuck all when a little girl needs your help. I say
for her to come over to the house tonight and that the three
of us will sit down and talk about it. Me, her and Mal. That
we'll work it out. Siobhan says that she will. She asks me to
tell her dad. Of course I say. She says thanks Mam. I say to
try and get her head down for a few hours. We'll be home by
the afternoon. Back in Limerick. The city of love. She hangs
up. I walk on. Towards the hotel.

I must find Mal. I am needed. I have to stay. She has never
needed me like this before. Not since she learned how to
crawl. So I won't be goin' anywhere. Breffni flashes into me
head . . . His naked body lying back in the bed. How fucking
great to be with that. To feel that again. But the Breff is the
Breff, with his new life and his imagined Nirvana in Kerry
and I think of him and smile sadly because it's a physical
need I have for him . . . that's it. I wish him well but deep
down I know he'll settle for drinking. He'll drink until he
can't drink anymore. I wonder how long he'll wait in the
square before he gives up on me. He'll drive off into the
sunset until some other whim hits him and he's off
somewhere else. He'll never stop to settle but I have. Me,
Mal and Siobhan. My family. But where is Mal? I still can't
find Mal. He'll turn up. Maybe this is what the fifty-plus
years have been leading up to. Minding your own flesh and
blood in her hour of need and helping her make a decision
or maybe taking care of a grandchild. A gift. Can't wait to tell
Mal. My pal. Where the fuck is he? I go inside the hotel
lobby and go up to the receptionist. I am suddenly stumped
at what I want to ask her so I say, I smile and I say, 'I wonder
could you help me but I seem to have lost my husband.'

End.

Discover. Read. Listen. Watch.

A NEW WAY TO ENGAGE WITH PLAYS

This award-winning digital library features over
3,000 playtexts, 400 audio plays, 300 hours
of video and 360 scholarly books.

Playtexts published by Methuen Drama,
The Arden Shakespeare, Faber & Faber,
Playwrights Canada Press, Aurora Metro Books
and Nick Hern Books.

Audio Plays from L.A. Theatre Works featuring
classic and modern works from the oeuvres
of leading American playwrights.

Video collections including films of live performances
from the RSC, The Globe and The National Theatre,
as well as acting masterclasses and BBC
feature films and documentaries.

FIND OUT MORE:
www.dramaonlinelibrary.com • ☑ @dramaonlinelib

For a complete listing of
Methuen Drama titles, visit:
www.bloomsbury.com/drama

Follow us on Twitter and keep up to date
with our news and publications
@MethuenDrama